Finding Out Who God Really Is

Children's Christianity Books

BABY PROFESSOR

EDUCATION KIDS

Speedy Publishing LLC
40 E. Main St. #1156
Newark, DE 19711
www.speedypublishing.com

Do you believe in God and appreciate His creations? But why can't we see him? We can't see God but we can feel His presence, for he lives in our hearts. We can also learn the good deeds and teachings of Jesus, and Jesus is God.

Kids, in this book you will learn interesting information about our ultimate Creator. Who is God really?

As part of our
religious and
spiritual training,
we study dramatic
scriptural accounts
about God. In this
way, we strengthen
our faith in Him
as our creator.

In our existence, we encounter the truth of God's words and the gift of His Son, which leads us to understand God's message to us. God becoming human in Jesus is a very important part of God's revelation to humankind.

Jesus is the son of God and part of God. He is both human and God. Being human, Jesus can relate to us and understand our feelings. Jesus is the greatest expression of God's love to us. In Jesus, God opens a path so we can come close to him.

Jesus came into this world through Mary. That is why Jesus is considered as both man and God.

As part of humanity, Jesus experienced suffering, pain, joy, and rejection. However, even though he was human, He remained holy for He never sinned against God, His father. Jesus came into the world to show us what God is like.

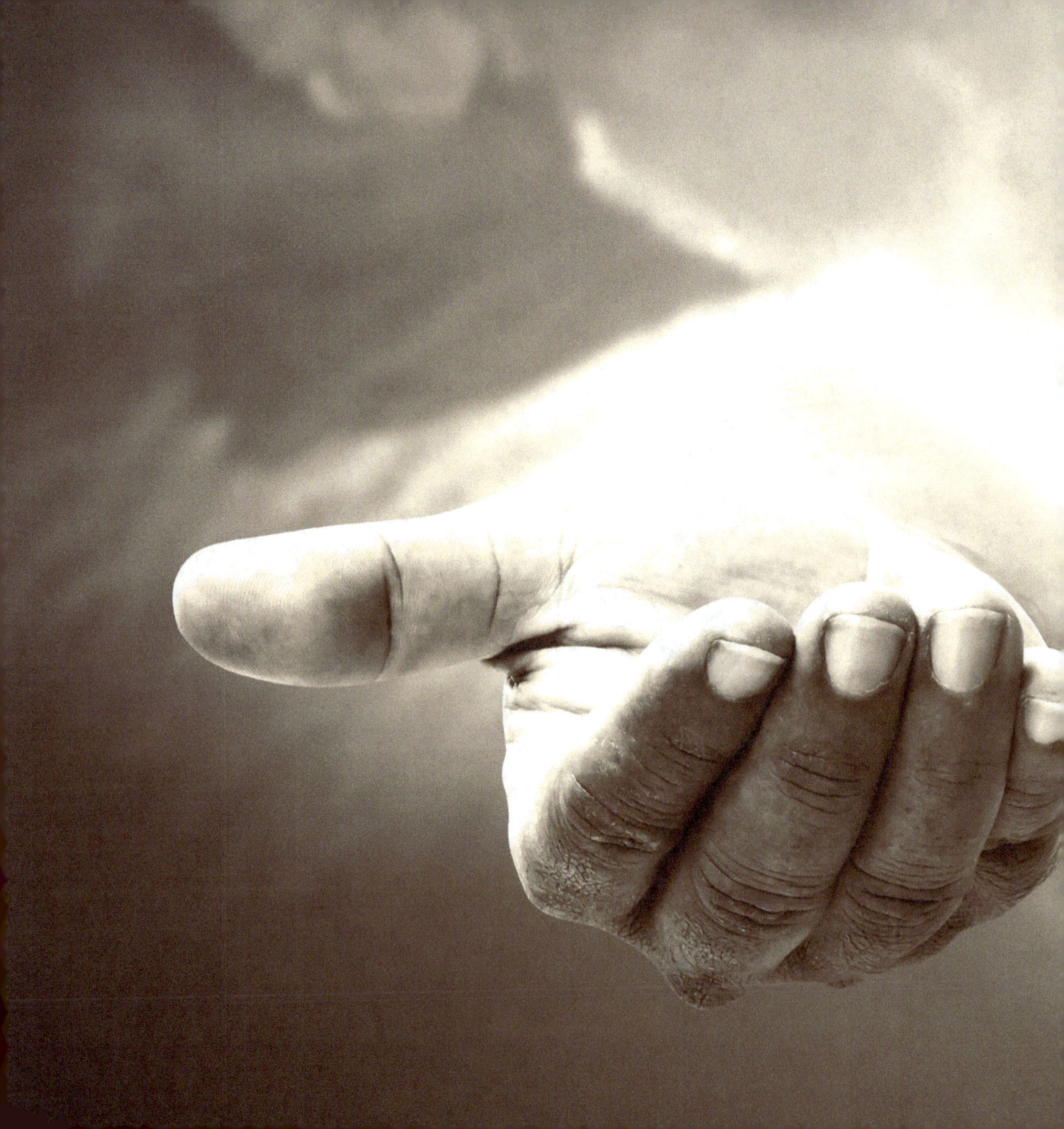

Why can't
we see God?
Where is He?

We can't see God, but we can feel His presence. God is everywhere and everything exists because of Him. Although we can't talk to Him face to face like we can talk to our friends, we can talk with Him and grow toward him wherever we are.

God knows what we are doing and what is in our hearts. He knows everything about us. We can learn more about God by reading His words in the Bible. We grow towards God by using what we learn from the Bible in our lives.

What does
God look like?

As humans, we cannot see God as we can see other people. Saint Paul says when we try to see God in our lives, it is like trying to look at the world using an old, broken mirror. But God calls us to Him, and Saint Paul says one day we will meet God face to face. God is always present in us, and is always calling to us. If we seek him by repenting our sins, and by good deeds while on earth and toward other people, we will draw closer to him.

Why can't
I hear God
talking to me?

God spoke directly to Moses and other prophets, and Jesus, son of God, spoke to thousands of people. In our times, we can still hear God's words through the Bible, which records what was said. Reading the Bible is a little like hearing the voice of God.

Who made
God? God is
the Alpha and
the Omega.

Knowing that God is the creator of everything, who then created Him? Did He create Himself for us? No, God was not created. He has always existed. He is the beginning and the end (the Alpha and Omega, which are the first and last letters of the Greek alphabet) of all things.

As the Bible tells us, in the beginning God created: heaven and the earth and all living things. God already existed before all those things, and makes all things possible. All His creations show us His power, goodness and wisdom.

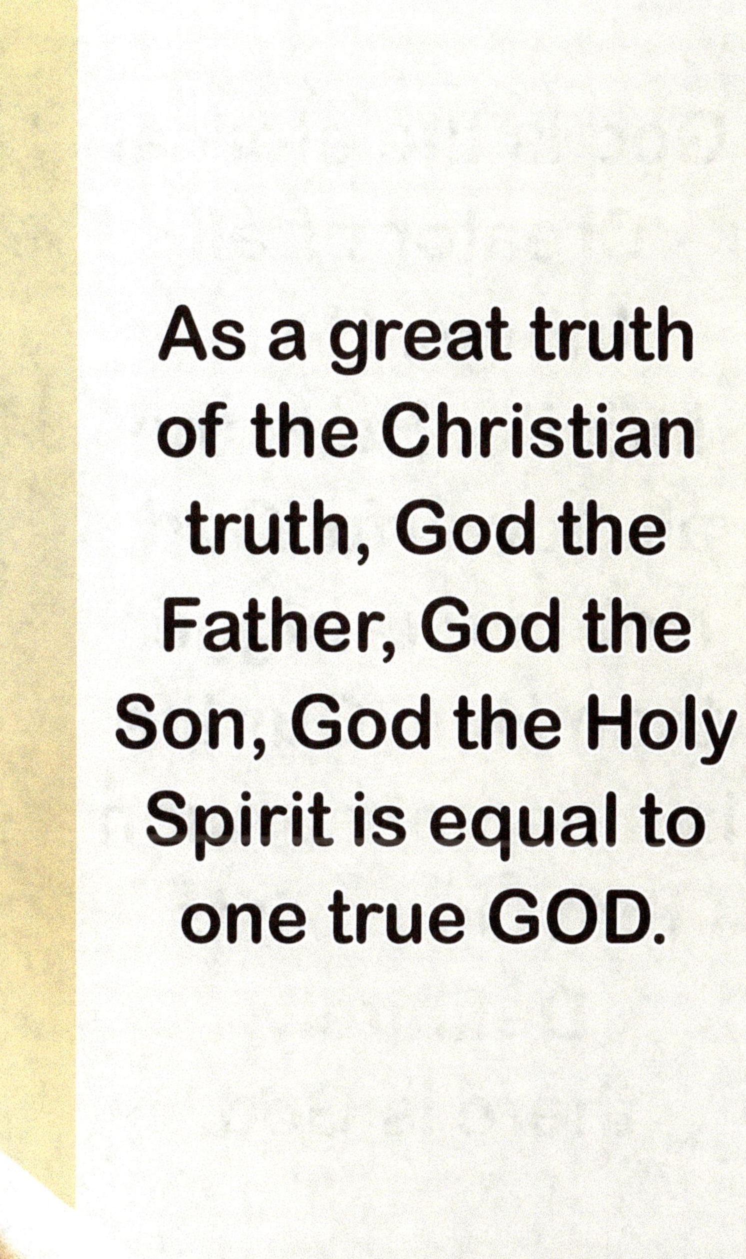
As a great truth
of the Christian
truth, God the
Father, God the
Son, God the Holy
Spirit is equal to
one true GOD.

God is the eternal Creator of all things. He is infinite. He is the all-powerful God. Nothing is bigger than Him. Our life is a demonstration that God exists. Definitely, there is God.

Visit

BABY PROFESSOR
EDUCATION KIDS

www.BabyProfessorBooks.com

to download Free Baby Professor eBooks
and view our catalog of new and exciting
Children's Books

www.ingramcontent.com/pod-product-compliance
Lightning Source LLC
Chambersburg PA
CBHW060619120726
48002CB00010B/3033